All rights reserved. Ruth Byrnes registered trademark.

Copyright Ruth Byrnes.

Disclaimer: The information presented in this text about the Law of Attraction is for general informational purposes only. It is not intended as professional advice and should not be interpreted as such. The Law of Attraction is a concept that may have different interpretations and outcomes for individuals. The effectiveness and results may vary depending on personal beliefs, attitudes, and actions. It is always recommended to consult with qualified professionals or seek appropriate guidance before making any significant changes in your life based on the concepts discussed in this text. The author and publisher disclaim any liability for any direct, indirect, or consequential loss or damage arising from the use or reliance upon any information provided in this text. The readers are solely responsible for their interpretation and application of the ideas presented in this text.

The new quality of time is change.

The world we consider so solidly true is a shadow we can pass through at any moment.

RUTH BYRNES

Manifesting Magic Empower Your Desires with Affirmations for Transformation

I

Introduction to the Benefits of Positive Affirmations in Daily Life.

Welcome to a world of positivity and self-empowerment! In this fast-paced and often challenging life, it's crucial to recognize the impact of our thoughts and beliefs on our overall well-being. Positive affirmations, simple yet powerful statements, can transform the way we perceive ourselves and the world around us.

By consciously repeating positive affirmations, we can rewire our minds, replace negative self-talk with self-encouragement, and cultivate a mindset of optimism and possibility. These affirmations act as a beacon of light, guiding us towards personal growth, resilience, and a more fulfilling life.

Through this journey, we will explore the profound benefits of integrating positive affirmations into our daily routine. From enhancing self-confidence and reducing stress to attracting abundance and manifesting our dreams, positive affirmations have the potential to shape our reality and unlock our true potential.

So, join us as we delve into the transformative power of positive affirmations and discover how they can uplift our spirits, cultivate gratitude, and create a positive ripple effect in every aspect of our lives. Get ready to embrace the extraordinary possibilities that await when we harness the power of positive thinking and affirmations.

Are you ready to embark on this empowering journey? Let's dive in and unlock the limitless potential within ourselves through the practice of positive affirmations.

The Benefits of Positive Affirmations:

1. Empowers and Uplifts: Positive affirmations have the power to uplift our spirits and boost our self-confidence. By consciously repeating affirmations like "I am capable," "I am deserving," or "I am enough," we cultivate a positive self-image and develop a resilient mindset.

2. Shifts Mindset and Perspective: Affirmations help us shift from negative thought patterns to positive ones. By replacing self-limiting beliefs with empowering statements, we rewire our minds to focus on possibilities, opportunities, and solutions.

3. Enhances Self-Confidence: Regularly practicing positive affirmations builds a strong sense of self-

confidence. Affirmations like "I believe in myself," "I trust my abilities," and "I am confident in my choices" help us overcome self-doubt and step into our true potential.

4. Reduces Stress and Anxiety: Positive affirmations can help reduce stress and anxiety by promoting a sense of calm and inner peace. Affirmations like "I am calm," "I am at peace," or "I release all worries" create a positive shift in our emotional state, allowing us to navigate challenges with greater ease.

The Benefits of Visualization:

1. Strengthens Goal Setting: Visualization is a powerful tool for manifesting our desires and achieving our goals. By visualizing ourselves successfully accomplishing our goals, we create a clear mental image of what we want to achieve, which enhances motivation and focus.

2. Enhances Performance: Athletes, artists, and professionals often use visualization techniques to enhance performance. By mentally rehearsing specific actions or scenarios, we improve our skills, build confidence, and increase the likelihood of success.

3. Activates the Subconscious Mind: Visualization accesses the power of the subconscious mind, which plays a significant role in shaping our reality. When we

vividly imagine our desired outcomes, our subconscious mind starts working towards manifesting them, attracting opportunities and synchronicities.

4. Boosts Positivity and Resilience: Visualization helps us cultivate a positive and resilient mindset. By visualizing positive outcomes and imagining ourselves overcoming challenges, we develop a sense of optimism and belief in our ability to navigate any situation.

By integrating positive affirmations and visualization practices into our lives, we unlock the potential to transform our mindset, manifest our dreams, and create a more positive and fulfilling reality. These practices empower us to become the architects of our own lives and embrace the limitless possibilities that lie within us.

Repeating positive affirmations to oneself means using words and phrases that express positive thoughts and emotions about oneself, one's life, and one's circumstances. These affirmations are intentional and aim to replace limiting or negative beliefs with empowered and confident thoughts.

When we repeat positive affirmations, we seek to create a positive and encouraging inner dialogue. For example, we might repeat phrases like "I am filled with confidence and determination," "I deserve success and happiness," or "I am capable of overcoming any obstacle." These affirmations help to reprogram our subconscious mind and reinforce positive beliefs about ourselves and our abilities.

The practice of repeating positive affirmations can have several benefits, including:

1. Boosting self-confidence: Affirmations help to instill a sense of self-belief and confidence, reminding us of our strengths and capabilities.

2. Shifting mindset: By replacing negative or self-limiting thoughts with positive ones, affirmations can help us adopt a more optimistic and empowered mindset.

3. Enhancing motivation: Positive affirmations can serve as a powerful motivator, inspiring us to take action towards our goals and dreams.

4. Improving self-esteem: Affirmations promote self-acceptance and self-love, fostering a positive self-image and increasing self-esteem.

5. Managing stress and anxiety: Regularly practicing positive affirmations can help reduce stress levels and alleviate anxiety by promoting a more positive outlook and mindset.

Remember, the key to effective affirmation practice is consistency and belief. By incorporating positive affirmations into your daily routine and truly embracing their messages, you can harness their transformative power and create a more positive and fulfilling life.

You are right in pointing out that the subconscious mind does not distinguish between what is true and what we tell it. The subconscious mind is deeply influenced by the information and messages it receives, both from external sources and from within ourselves.

When we repeat positive affirmations to ourselves, we are intentionally sending messages to our subconscious mind. These affirmations can help reprogram our subconscious beliefs and thoughts, replacing negative or limiting beliefs with positive and empowering ones.

By consistently repeating positive affirmations, we can shift our mindset and perspective. This can lead to changes in our behavior, emotions, and overall well-being. Positive affirmations can help increase our self-confidence, boost our motivation, reduce stress and anxiety, improve our relationships, and enhance our overall mindset and outlook on life.

The power of positive affirmations lies in their ability to rewire our subconscious mind and align it with our conscious desires and goals. They help us focus on the positive aspects of ourselves and our lives, and they reinforce beliefs that support our growth and success.

It's important to note that while positive affirmations can be a powerful tool, they work best when combined with consistent action and a belief in their effectiveness. It's about cultivating a positive mindset and taking inspired action towards our goals.

In summary, repeating positive affirmations can bring about positive changes in ourselves by reprogramming our subconscious mind, shifting our perspective, and aligning our beliefs with our desires and goals.

Visualization is the process of mentally creating vivid images in our mind. It is a practice that involves using our imagination to generate a detailed mental representation of what we want to manifest in reality.

When we visualize effectively, we fully immerse ourselves in our imagination, creating clear, vibrant images that evoke the desired experiences and outcomes. It goes beyond simply thinking about something; it's about engaging all our senses to make the mental imagery as real and vivid as possible.

The power of visualization lies in its ability to communicate with our subconscious mind. Our subconscious doesn't distinguish between what is real and what we tell it. By consistently visualizing our desired outcomes, we are effectively programming our subconscious mind to align with those desires.

Through visualization, we can enhance our focus, motivation, and belief in achieving our goals. It helps us develop a clear mental blueprint of our desired future, allowing us to align our thoughts, actions, and behaviors accordingly. By consistently visualizing success, we cultivate a positive mindset and attract opportunities and resources that align with our visions.

In summary, visualization is a powerful technique that harnesses the creative power of our imagination to manifest our goals and desires. It allows us to communicate with our subconscious mind and align our thoughts and actions with our desired outcomes. By practicing visualization regularly, we can tap into our innate potential and create the life we envision.

"I am confident, capable, and deserving of success in every area of my life."

By consistently repeating this affirmation, you are programming your subconscious mind to believe in your own abilities and worthiness. This affirmation can help boost your confidence, enhance your self-belief, and attract opportunities for success in various aspects of your life.

Remember, the key to effective affirmation is repetition and emotional engagement. By repeating positive statements like this one regularly and with genuine conviction, you can gradually rewire your subconscious mind to align with your desired outcome. This can lead to increased self-confidence, improved performance, and a more positive mindset, ultimately bringing about the desired results you seek.

"I am a magnet for wealth and abundance. Money flows to me effortlessly and abundantly."

By repeating this affirmation regularly, you are programming your subconscious mind to believe in your ability to attract and receive financial abundance. This affirmation can help shift your mindset from scarcity to abundance, opening yourself up to opportunities and allowing money to flow into your life with ease.

Remember, the key to effective affirmations is belief and emotional resonance. As you repeat this affirmation, imagine the feeling of abundance and visualize yourself enjoying financial prosperity. By consistently reinforcing this positive belief, you can cultivate a prosperity mindset and attract the abundance you desire.

It's important to note that affirmations work best when combined with inspired action. Alongside repeating this affirmation, take proactive steps towards your financial goals, such as budgeting, saving, and pursuing opportunities for growth. This combination of positive affirmation and aligned action can help manifest the financial results you desire.

"I am deserving of a deep and loving relationship. I attract a partner who loves and respects me for who I am."

By repeating this affirmation, you are affirming your worthiness and openness to receiving a loving relationship. This affirmation can help shift your mindset from any limiting beliefs or past experiences and create space for love to enter your life.

As you repeat this affirmation, visualize yourself in a loving and fulfilling relationship. Imagine the feelings of love, joy, and connection that come with being in a healthy partnership. Embrace the belief that you deserve love and that the right partner is on their way to you.

While affirmations are a powerful tool, it's important to remember that they are most effective when combined with self-love, personal growth, and taking positive action. Be open to opportunities to meet new people, practice self-care, and cultivate a loving relationship with yourself. By aligning your thoughts, beliefs, and actions, you can manifest a loving relationship that is in alignment with your desires and values.

"I am grateful for my vibrant health and my body's ability to heal and thrive. I make choices that nourish and support my physical and mental well-being."

By repeating this affirmation, you are affirming your gratitude for your health and setting the intention to make choices that contribute to your well-being. This affirmation can help shift your mindset towards a proactive and positive approach to your health.

As you repeat this affirmation, visualize yourself in a state of optimal health. Imagine yourself full of vitality, energy, and vitality. Embrace the belief that your body has a natural ability to heal and rejuvenate itself.

In addition to affirmations, it's important to take actions that support your health, such as maintaining a balanced diet, exercising regularly, getting enough rest, and seeking appropriate medical care when needed.

Combine your affirmations with healthy habits and self-care practices to enhance your overall well-being.

Remember, affirmations are a tool to support and reinforce positive beliefs and mindset. They work best when used consistently and in conjunction with a holistic approach to health and well-being.

1. Confidence: By consistently repeating affirmations like "I am confident and capable," we can boost our self-esteem and develop a stronger belief in our abilities. This can help us overcome self-doubt and approach challenges with a more positive mindset.

2. Motivation: Affirmations such as "I am driven and motivated to achieve my goals" can help us stay focused and determined. By reinforcing these positive beliefs, we can cultivate a sense of purpose and enthusiasm that propels us forward in our endeavors.

3. Resilience: When faced with setbacks or obstacles, repeating affirmations like "I am resilient and can overcome any challenge" can strengthen our mental resilience. It reminds us that setbacks are temporary and encourages us to persist and find solutions.

4. Positivity: Affirmations focused on positive thinking, such as "I choose to see the good in every situation," help reframe our perspective and cultivate a more optimistic outlook. This can enhance our overall well-

being and help us maintain a positive attitude even in difficult times.

5. Stress Reduction: Affirmations like "I am calm and centered in every situation" can help reduce stress and promote relaxation. By consciously repeating these affirmations, we can train our minds to respond to stressors in a calmer and more composed manner.

Remember, the effectiveness of affirmations lies in repetition and belief. Consistently repeating positive affirmations helps rewire our thought patterns and replace negative self-talk with empowering and supportive language. By embracing the power of positive affirmations, we can create a more positive and fulfilling life experience.

Here are a few examples:

1. Grace is a talented baker who creates delicious pastries and cakes that bring joy to people's lives.

2. Alex is a skilled musician who captivates audiences with their soulful melodies and powerful performances.

3. Emma is a compassionate nurse who provides comfort and care to patients in need.

4. Liam is a dedicated teacher who inspires his students to love learning and reach their full potential.

5. Sophia is a talented artist whose paintings evoke emotions and tell captivating stories.

6. Ethan is a passionate environmentalist who works tirelessly to protect and preserve our planet.

7. Olivia is a charismatic leader who motivates and empowers her team to achieve great success.

8. Henry is a gifted writer who crafts compelling stories that transport readers to different worlds.

9. Ava is a skilled athlete who pushes her limits and constantly strives for excellence in her sport.

10. Noah is a visionary entrepreneur who brings innovative ideas to life and creates impactful businesses.

These examples highlight individuals and their respective talents or qualities, showcasing the positive aspects of their identities.

Here are some examples of well-known individuals who have used positive affirmations or repeated empowering statements:

1. Oprah Winfrey: "I am enough. I have everything I need within me to create the life I desire."

2. Will Smith: "I am in control of my thoughts and emotions. I choose positivity and success in every aspect of my life."

3. Serena Williams: "I am a champion. I am strong, powerful, and unstoppable on and off the court."

4. Elon Musk: "I am a visionary. I have the ability to change the world and make a positive impact through my ideas and innovations."

5. Michelle Obama: "I am capable and deserving of success. I use my voice to empower and inspire others."

6. Dwayne "The Rock" Johnson: "I am relentless in my pursuit of greatness. I overcome obstacles and achieve my goals with unwavering determination."

7. Beyoncé: "I am confident and unapologetically myself. I embrace my uniqueness and use my talents to uplift others."

8. Tony Robbins: "I am the creator of my destiny. I have the power to shape my life and achieve unlimited success."

9. J.K. Rowling: "I am a talented storyteller. My imagination knows no bounds, and my words have the power to inspire millions."

10. Nelson Mandela: "I am the master of my fate. I am resilient, and I can bring about positive change even in the face of adversity."

These individuals have demonstrated the power of positive self-talk and affirmations in their personal and professional lives. They have used these empowering statements to overcome challenges, achieve success, and inspire others.

Of course! Here's an encouragement for the reader to embrace their inner power and become the protagonist of their own life:

"Dear reader, you hold within you the immense power to shape your own destiny. You have unique talents, dreams, and aspirations that are waiting to be unleashed. Embrace your journey with courage, determination, and a belief in your own abilities.

Remember, you are the author of your story. Take charge, make bold choices, and don't be afraid to take risks. Trust in your instincts, listen to your heart, and let your passion guide you.

Know that challenges are opportunities in disguise, and with every setback, you grow stronger and wiser. Keep pushing forward, even when faced with obstacles, for they are mere stepping stones on your path to success.

Believe in yourself and your dreams. Dare to dream big and work diligently towards their realization. Surround yourself with positivity, support, and like-minded individuals who uplift and inspire you.

You have the power to create a life that is meaningful, fulfilling, and aligned with your deepest desires. Embrace your uniqueness, embrace your strengths, and step into the spotlight as the protagonist of your own extraordinary journey.

So go forth with confidence, resilience, and a sense of adventure. Embrace the challenges, celebrate the victories, and cherish every moment along the way.

Your story is waiting to be written, and I believe in your ability to make it extraordinary.

You are the protagonist of your life's story, and the world eagerly awaits the greatness that you will bring. Believe in yourself, embrace your power, and let your light shine brightly. Your time is now, and I know you will seize it with courage and grace."

Remember, you are capable of achieving remarkable things. Keep believing in yourself and never stop pursuing your dreams.

II

Visualization is a powerful technique that involves creating clear and vivid mental images of your desired reality. It is based on the belief that the mind and body are interconnected, and by visualizing positive outcomes, you can influence your thoughts, emotions, and actions, leading to the manifestation of your desires.

Here are step-by-step processes and methods for effective visualization:

1. Relaxation: Begin by finding a quiet and comfortable space where you can relax. Take deep breaths to calm your mind and body, and release any tension or stress.

2. Setting Intentions: Clearly define what you want to visualize and set your intentions for the practice. Be specific about your desired outcome and focus on positive aspects.

3. Creating Mental Images: Close your eyes and start to imagine the scene or situation as vividly as possible. Use your imagination to see, hear, and feel the details of your desired reality. Engage all your senses to make the visualization more immersive.

4. Emotional Engagement: As you visualize, evoke the emotions and feelings associated with achieving your desired outcome. Allow yourself to experience joy, gratitude, excitement, or any positive emotions that align with your vision.

5. Repetition and Consistency: Practice visualization regularly to reinforce the desired image in your mind. The more you repeat the visualization, the more it becomes ingrained in your subconscious.

6. Believe and Let Go: Have faith in the process and trust that your visualizations will manifest. Release any doubts or attachment to the outcome and surrender to the universe's timing.

Remember, visualization is a personal practice, and everyone may have their unique methods and techniques. Find what works best for you and be consistent in your practice. With dedication and belief, visualization can be a powerful tool for manifesting your dreams and goals.

Yes, it is true that it is recommended to visualize in the first person when practicing visualization. This means imagining yourself living and experiencing your desire firsthand, as if it has already been realized. This approach creates a deeper emotional involvement and enhances the effectiveness of visualization.

By visualizing in the first person, you put yourself in an active perspective and actively participate in the desired situation or experience. Imagine seeing through your own eyes, feeling through your own senses, and acting as if you are in the scene. This personal engagement helps align your subconscious mind with your desires and reinforces the belief that your dreams are within reach. So, immerse yourself fully in the visualization process and let your imagination take you on a journey of manifestation and fulfillment.

Including emotions in your visualization can greatly enhance its effectiveness. Emotions add depth and intensity to your visualizations, making them more vivid and impactful.

When you visualize, imagine not only the visuals but also the accompanying emotions. Feel the joy, excitement, and fulfillment as if your desired outcome has already manifested. Allow yourself to experience the positive emotions associated with achieving your goals or living your dream life.

By incorporating emotions into your visualization, you are signaling to your subconscious mind the intensity of your desires and reinforcing the belief that what you are visualizing is not only possible but also deeply meaningful to you. This emotional engagement helps to align your thoughts, feelings, and actions with your desired outcomes, increasing the likelihood of manifesting them in your reality.

So, as you visualize, let the emotions flow naturally and fully immerse yourself in the positive feelings associated with your desired experiences. This will amplify the power of your visualizations and support you in attracting and manifesting what you truly desire.

The emotions to include in visualization depend on each individual's goals and desires. However, there are some common positive emotions that are often associated with the process of visualization. Here are some of them:

1. Joy: Feeling deep joy in visualizing what you desire helps you connect with the happiness you would experience upon achieving your goals.

2. Gratitude: Having gratitude for what you already have and for what you are about to manifest helps create a positive and open mindset towards abundance.

3. Confidence: Nurturing a strong belief in yourself and your abilities allows you to visualize with a sense of security and determination.

4. Love: Including love in your visualization helps you create a deep emotional connection with what you desire, stimulating greater motivation and engagement.

5. Excitement: Feeling a sense of excitement and adventure while visualizing stimulates enthusiasm and positive energy, encouraging perseverance and action.

6. Satisfaction: Imagining the sense of satisfaction and fulfillment you would experience upon achieving your goals helps you visualize with a sense of completeness and success.

Remember that each person may have different emotions that are meaningful to them. Choose the emotions that resonate with you and help you feel in tune with the fulfillment of your desires.

The most powerful emotion can vary from person to person, as everyone may react differently to emotions. However, some of the emotions that are generally considered powerful include:

1. Love: Love is a powerful emotion that can drive people to do extraordinary things. It can provide a sense of deep connection, compassion, and joy.

2. Joy: Joy is a powerful and uplifting emotion that brings happiness, excitement, and a sense of fulfillment. It can inspire enthusiasm, positivity, and a zest for life.

3. Gratitude: Gratitude is a powerful emotion that cultivates a sense of appreciation and thankfulness. It can enhance overall well-being, promote positive relationships, and foster resilience.

4. Empathy: Empathy is a powerful emotion that allows us to understand and share the feelings of others. It

promotes compassion, kindness, and a sense of unity with others.

5. Determination: Determination is a powerful emotion that fuels motivation and perseverance. It helps us overcome obstacles, achieve goals, and reach our full potential.

Remember, the power of an emotion lies in how it is experienced and expressed by each individual.

Love is often considered the most powerful emotion because of its profound impact on individuals and the world around them. Here are a few reasons why love is often seen as the most powerful emotion:

1. Connection: Love creates a deep sense of connection and bond between individuals. It goes beyond superficial interactions and allows people to form strong emotional attachments and relationships.

2. Compassion and Empathy: Love enables individuals to feel compassion and empathy towards others. It encourages acts of kindness, understanding, and support, fostering a sense of unity and belonging.

3. Motivation: Love can be a powerful motivator, driving individuals to take actions and make sacrifices for the well-being of loved ones. It can inspire selflessness, determination, and a willingness to go above and beyond.

4. Healing and Growth: Love has the power to heal emotional wounds and promote personal growth. It provides a nurturing and supportive environment where individuals can feel accepted, valued, and encouraged to become the best versions of themselves.

5. Happiness and Fulfillment: Love brings happiness, joy, and a sense of fulfillment. It can create meaningful experiences and memories, enhance overall well-being, and provide a sense of purpose and meaning in life.

It's important to note that the power of love lies not only in romantic relationships but also in the love we feel for family, friends, community, and even humanity as a whole. Love has the ability to transform lives, inspire positive change, and create a more compassionate and harmonious world.

III

Here are 20 positive affirmations that can have a transformative impact on one's life:

1. I am worthy of love, happiness, and success.

2. I am capable of achieving my goals and dreams.

3. I attract positive opportunities and abundance into my life.

4. I radiate confidence and believe in my abilities.

5. I am grateful for all the blessings in my life.

6. I embrace change and see it as an opportunity for growth.

7. I release all negativity and embrace positivity in every aspect of my life.

8. I am surrounded by loving and supportive relationships.

9. I am deserving of good health and take care of my mind, body, and spirit.

10. I am resilient and overcome challenges with grace and determination.

11. I trust in the process of life and know that everything happens for my highest good.

12. I forgive myself and others, and release any resentment or grudges.

13. I choose to focus on the present moment and find joy in the little things.

14. I am open to receiving love, abundance, and all the good that life has to offer.

15. I am the creator of my own reality and have the power to manifest my desires.

16. I choose thoughts that uplift and inspire me.

17. I am confident in expressing my true self and embracing my uniqueness.

18. I am worthy of success and prosperity in all areas of my life.

19. I attract positive and supportive people who inspire and motivate me.

20. I am filled with love, peace, and happiness, and I radiate that energy out into the world.

Remember, repetition and belief are key when using affirmations. Consistently repeating these affirmations with conviction can help reprogram your subconscious mind and bring about positive changes in your life.

Here are 20 affirmations focused on love:

1. I am worthy of love and deserving of a healthy, fulfilling relationship.

2. Love flows effortlessly into my life.

3. I attract loving and supportive people into my life.

4. I am open to giving and receiving love unconditionally.

5. I radiate love and compassion towards myself and others.

6. I am deserving of a passionate and joyful love.

7. My heart is open to new love experiences and opportunities.

8. I release any past hurt and make space for love to enter my life.

9. I am grateful for the love that surrounds me every day.

10. I am a magnet for love and my soulmate is on their way to me.

11. Love comes to me easily and naturally.

12. I attract a loving and nurturing partner who cherishes and respects me.

13. I am confident and authentic in expressing my love.

14. I create a loving and harmonious relationship with my partner.

15. I am worthy of deep, meaningful connections and soulful love.

16. I am deserving of love, and I allow it to flow abundantly in my life.

17. I release any fear of love and trust in the process of love unfolding.

18. I am grateful for the lessons and growth that love brings into my life.

19. Love fills every aspect of my life, bringing me joy and fulfillment.

20. I am a source of love and happiness, and I attract the same into my life.

Remember to repeat these affirmations regularly, believe in them, and align your thoughts and actions with the energy of love. Embracing a positive mindset about love can help attract and manifest beautiful love experiences in your life.

Here are 20 affirmations focused on abundance and prosperity:

1. I am worthy of abundant wealth and success.

2. Money comes to me easily and effortlessly.

3. I am a magnet for financial abundance and opportunities.

4. I release all limiting beliefs about money and embrace my ability to attract wealth.

5. I am grateful for the abundance that flows into my life.

6. I am open to receiving infinite possibilities for financial growth.

7. I attract lucrative opportunities and prosperous ventures.

8. I am financially free, and my income is constantly increasing.

9. I use money wisely to create a life of abundance and joy.

10. I deserve to be prosperous and enjoy the fruits of my hard work.

11. I am a money magnet, and wealth flows to me from multiple sources.

12. I release any fears or blocks that hinder my financial success.

13. I am aligned with the energy of abundance, and it manifests in all areas of my life.

14. I am open to receiving unexpected financial blessings.

15. I attract and manifest abundance effortlessly.

16. I am a wise steward of my finances, and money works for me.

17. My bank account is constantly growing, and I am financially secure.

18. I have an abundance mindset, and I attract wealth with ease.

19. Money flows to me in expected and unexpected ways.

20. I am grateful for the abundance that surrounds me, and I attract more of it into my life.

Remember to repeat these affirmations regularly, believe in them, and take inspired actions towards your financial goals. Aligning your thoughts and beliefs with the energy of abundance can help attract wealth and financial prosperity into your life.

Here are 20 affirmations focused on health and well-being:

1. I am in perfect health and vitality.

2. My body is strong, and I feel energized every day.

3. I nourish my body with healthy and nutritious foods.

4. I am grateful for my body's ability to heal and rejuvenate.

5. Every cell in my body radiates with health and vitality.

6. I embrace a healthy lifestyle that supports my well-being.

7. I attract and manifest vibrant health in all aspects of my life.

8. I am worthy of optimal health and well-being.

9. My immune system is strong, and I easily ward off illness.

10. I listen to my body's needs and give it the care it deserves.

11. I release any negativity or stress that may affect my health.

12. I am in harmony with my body, mind, and spirit.

13. I attract positive and healing energies into my life.

14. I am grateful for the abundance of natural resources that support my well-being.

15. My body heals quickly and efficiently.

16. I radiate love and kindness, which contribute to my overall health.

17. I am proactive in taking care of my physical, mental, and emotional well-being.

18. I am surrounded by loving and supportive people who encourage my health goals.

19. I embrace a balanced and harmonious lifestyle.

20. Every day, in every way, I am getting healthier and stronger.

Remember to affirm these statements regularly, believe in your body's innate ability to heal and thrive, and take actions that support your overall well-being. Combine these affirmations with healthy habits and a positive mindset, and you'll be on your way to experiencing vibrant health.

Here are 20 affirmations focused on having a large and loving family and children:

1. My family is expanding with love, joy, and laughter.

2. I am open to receiving the blessings of a large and happy family.

3. I am surrounded by loving and supportive family members.

4. I attract a loving partner who shares my desire for a large family.

5. I am grateful for the gift of parenthood and the joy it brings.

6. My home is filled with the love and laughter of my children.

7. I am deserving of a beautiful and fulfilling family life.

8. I have an abundance of love to give to my children.

9. I create a nurturing and supportive environment for my family to thrive.

10. I attract positive and loving relationships with my children.

11. I am a patient and loving parent, guiding my children with compassion.

12. I am financially abundant and able to provide for my growing family.

13. I am surrounded by a strong support system to help raise my children.

14. I am capable of balancing the responsibilities of parenthood with grace.

15. I trust in divine timing for the arrival of each child into my life.

16. I am blessed with healthy and happy pregnancies.

17. My home is filled with warmth, love, and sibling bonds.

18. I attract like-minded friends who also desire a large family.

19. I am open to receiving guidance and wisdom to be the best parent I can be.

20. My family is my greatest treasure, and I am grateful for their presence in my life.

Remember to repeat these affirmations regularly, believe in your ability to create the family life you desire, and take proactive steps to build and nurture your relationships. Trust in the journey and have faith that the universe will align to bring your desired family into your life.

Here are 20 affirmations focused on achieving professional success and building a fulfilling career:

1. I am highly skilled and capable in my field of expertise.

2. I attract abundant opportunities for growth and advancement in my career.

3. I am focused and determined to achieve my professional goals.

4. I am open to learning and continuously improving my skills.

5. I am confident in my abilities and trust in my potential for success.

6. I am deserving of recognition and rewards for my hard work and dedication.

7. I am aligned with my passion and purpose, which drives my career success.

8. I attract supportive mentors and allies who guide me on my career path.

9. I embrace challenges as opportunities for growth and development.

10. I am a valuable asset to any team or organization I work with.

11. I have a clear vision for my career and take consistent action towards its realization.

12. I am open to new possibilities and willing to step outside of my comfort zone.

13. I am a magnet for lucrative opportunities and financial abundance in my profession.

14. I radiate confidence and professionalism in all that I do.

15. I am grateful for the successes I have achieved and excited for future accomplishments.

16. I attract positive and fulfilling work experiences that align with my values.

17. I am a natural leader, inspiring and motivating others to achieve greatness.

18. I create a harmonious work-life balance that supports my overall well-being.

19. I am resilient in the face of challenges and bounce back stronger than ever.

20. I am living my dream career, enjoying both personal fulfillment and financial prosperity.

Repeat these affirmations daily, internalize their positive messages, and let them guide your thoughts and actions towards achieving professional success. Remember to take proactive steps towards your goals and remain persistent, knowing that success is within your reach.

Here are 20 affirmations focused on attracting a job that allows for travel and enriching experiences:

1. I am open to opportunities that combine my passion for travel with my professional skills.

2. I attract a job that allows me to explore the world and experience different cultures.

3. I am deserving of a career that offers exciting travel opportunities and new adventures.

4. I am ready to embrace new experiences and broaden my horizons through work-related travel.

5. I attract a job that provides a perfect balance between work and travel.

6. I am confident in my ability to excel in a job that requires frequent travel.

7. I attract opportunities that allow me to make meaningful connections with people from all over the world.

8. I am excited to immerse myself in different environments and learn from diverse perspectives.

9. I am grateful for the opportunities that come my way to travel while working.

10. I am aligned with a career that allows me to satisfy my wanderlust and fulfill my professional aspirations.

11. I am open to learning and growing through the experiences and challenges that come with travel.

12. I attract a job that values and supports my passion for exploration and discovery.

13. I embrace the freedom and flexibility that come with a career that involves travel.

14. I am adaptable and resourceful in navigating different cultures and environments.

15. I attract opportunities that combine my skills with my love for travel, creating a fulfilling career.

16. I am confident in my ability to create memorable experiences and make a positive impact through my work.

17. I am grateful for the personal and professional growth that comes with travel experiences.

18. I attract a job that allows me to expand my knowledge and skills while exploring new destinations.

19. I am excited about the possibilities that arise from having a job that involves travel.

20. I am living a life of adventure and fulfillment, combining my passion for travel with a successful career.

Repeat these affirmations regularly, visualize yourself in the job of your dreams, and take inspired action towards finding and securing opportunities that align with your desire for travel and enriching experiences. Trust that the universe will bring forth the right opportunities and that you have what it takes to create a career that allows you to explore the world.

Certainly! Here are 20 affirmations focused on embracing beauty and charm:

1. I radiate beauty and charm from within.

2. I am naturally beautiful, inside and out.

3. I am confident in my unique and captivating charm.

4. I am comfortable and confident in my own skin.

5. My inner beauty shines through in every interaction.

6. I attract positive attention with my irresistible charm.

7. I embrace and celebrate my own unique beauty.

8. I am deserving of love and admiration just as I am.

9. I exude confidence and grace in all that I do.

10. I am a magnet for beauty and elegance.

11. I embrace my flaws and see them as part of my unique charm.

12. I carry myself with poise and elegance.

13. I am grateful for the beauty that surrounds me and reflects back to me.

14. I nurture and take care of my physical and mental well-being.

15. I attract loving and supportive relationships with my magnetic charm.

16. I am a captivating presence that draws people towards me.

17. I embrace my individuality and let my inner beauty shine.

18. I choose to see and appreciate the beauty in others and myself.

19. I am confident in my own style and personal expression of beauty.

20. I embody beauty and charm effortlessly.

Repeat these affirmations regularly, internalize them, and believe in your own beauty and charm. Embrace and celebrate your unique qualities, and let your inner light shine brightly for the world to see. Remember, true beauty comes from within, and when you embrace and radiate that inner beauty, you naturally exude charm and captivate those around you.

In conclusion, it is important to recognize that the universe does not pass judgment on us or our actions. Instead, it reflects our innermost being. The universe is like a mirror that reflects back to us the energy and vibrations we emit. It responds to our thoughts, beliefs, and intentions, not based on any external judgment or evaluation.

This understanding is empowering because it reminds us that we have the ability to shape our reality through our thoughts, emotions, and actions. We are co-creators of our experiences, and by aligning ourselves with positive energy, love, and authenticity, we can attract and manifest the life we desire.

Therefore, let us release any feelings of judgment, comparison, or self-doubt. Instead, let us focus on nurturing our true selves, expressing our unique gifts, and living in alignment with our deepest values and desires. By doing so, we can create a reality that reflects our inner beauty, authenticity, and potential.

Remember, the universe supports and responds to our true essence. As we embrace and radiate our authentic self, we attract experiences, opportunities, and relationships that align with our highest good. Let us trust in the process, have faith in our journey, and embrace the infinite possibilities that lie before us.

IV

Here's an explanation on how to effectively visualize and create images in your mind:

1. Find a quiet and comfortable space where you can relax and focus your attention.

2. Close your eyes and take a few deep breaths to center yourself.

3. Begin by setting a clear intention for your visualization. What specific outcome or experience would you like to visualize?

4. Create a detailed mental image of what you desire to see or experience. Use your imagination to make the image as vivid and real as possible.

5. Engage your senses. Visualize not only what you see, but also what you hear, feel, taste, and smell in the scene. Make it a multi-sensory experience.

6. Embrace the emotions associated with your visualization. Feel the joy, excitement, and fulfillment as if you have already achieved your desired outcome.

7. Hold the image in your mind and immerse yourself in the experience. Allow yourself to fully believe in the reality of what you are visualizing.

8. Repeat this visualization practice regularly, ideally on a daily basis. Consistency is key in strengthening your visualization abilities.

9. Trust in the process and let go of any attachment to the outcome. Have faith that the universe will align with your intentions.

10. Take inspired action towards your goals and desires. Visualization alone is not enough; it should be complemented by proactive steps towards manifesting your visions.

Remember, effective visualization requires focus, belief, and emotional engagement. By consistently practicing visualization techniques, you can harness the power of your imagination to manifest your desires and create the life you envision.

Here's an example of how you can visualize getting married:

1. Find a quiet and comfortable space where you can relax and focus your attention.

2. Close your eyes and take a few deep breaths to center yourself.

3. Set the intention to visualize your ideal wedding day and the feeling of being happily married.

4. Imagine yourself walking down the aisle, surrounded by loved ones, towards your partner waiting at the altar.

5. Visualize the details of your wedding ceremony, such as the beautiful decorations, the music playing, and the joyful atmosphere.

6. Engage your senses by imagining the scent of flowers, the sound of laughter and celebration, and the touch of your partner's hand.

7. Feel the emotions of love, excitement, and deep connection as you exchange vows and rings with your partner.

8. See yourself celebrating with family and friends, dancing, and enjoying a memorable reception.

9. Hold onto the image of you and your partner standing together as a married couple, radiating happiness and love.

10. Express gratitude for this experience and visualize a happy and fulfilling life together.

Remember to repeat this visualization regularly and infuse it with positive emotions and belief. By consistently visualizing your ideal wedding day, you are aligning your energy and intentions with the desire to get married, increasing the likelihood of manifesting it in your life.

Here's an example of how you can visualize attracting wealth and abundance:

1. Find a quiet and comfortable space where you can relax and focus your attention.

2. Close your eyes and take a few deep breaths to center yourself.

3. Set the intention to visualize a life of financial abundance and prosperity.

4. Imagine yourself in a luxurious setting, surrounded by symbols of wealth and abundance, such as a beautiful mansion or a tropical paradise.

5. Visualize a specific amount of money that you desire to manifest, whether it's a specific sum or a general feeling of abundance.

6. See yourself receiving large amounts of money, whether through a successful business venture, a promotion, or unexpected opportunities.

7. Imagine the feeling of financial security and freedom that comes with having abundant resources at your disposal.

8. Engage your senses by visualizing the sights, sounds, and textures associated with wealth, such as the feeling

of crisp banknotes, the sound of clinking coins, or the sight of a bank account balance increasing.

9. Feel gratitude for the abundance flowing into your life and the opportunities it brings to create a positive impact in the world.

10. Repeat affirmations such as "I am open to receiving unlimited abundance," "Money flows to me effortlessly," and "I am a magnet for wealth and prosperity."

Remember to maintain a positive and abundant mindset as you visualize, and take inspired action towards your financial goals. Visualization is a powerful tool to align your thoughts, emotions, and actions with the manifestation of wealth and abundance in your life.

Here's an example of how you can visualize having a large family in a beautiful home:

1. Find a quiet and comfortable space where you can relax and focus your attention.

2. Close your eyes and take a few deep breaths to center yourself.

3. Set the intention to visualize a life with a loving and large family in a beautiful home.

4. Imagine yourself in a spacious and warm home, filled with laughter, love, and joy.

5. Visualize your family members, including your partner and children, playing and bonding together in various rooms of the house.

6. See each family member's smiling face, feel the love and connection between you all, and hear the sounds of laughter and happiness.

7. Picture yourself preparing meals and enjoying family dinners around a large dining table, creating lasting memories together.

8. Imagine the bedrooms, each uniquely decorated for your children, with their favorite toys and personal touches.

9. Visualize your home filled with love, harmony, and a sense of belonging.

10. Feel gratitude for the abundance of love and happiness that your large family and beautiful home bring into your life.

Continue to visualize this scene regularly, adding details and emotions that resonate with you. Allow yourself to feel the joy and fulfillment that comes with having a large and loving family in a beautiful home. Remember to align your thoughts, emotions, and actions with your visualization, taking steps to create the life you desire.

Here's an example of how you can visualize having an adventurous job that allows you to travel to exotic destinations:

1. Find a quiet and comfortable space where you can relax and focus your attention.

2. Close your eyes and take a few deep breaths to center yourself.

3. Set the intention to visualize a career that involves exciting adventures and traveling to exotic locations.

4. Picture yourself in different breathtaking destinations, such as tropical islands, ancient ruins, or bustling cities.

5. Visualize yourself fully immersed in your adventurous job, whether it's as a travel writer, photographer, or tour guide.

6. Imagine exploring new cultures, meeting interesting people, and experiencing thrilling activities in each location.

7. Feel the sense of freedom and excitement that comes with having a career that allows you to travel and discover the world.

8. Visualize yourself capturing stunning photographs, writing captivating stories, or guiding others through unforgettable experiences.

9. See yourself embracing the challenges and learning opportunities that come with traveling to new and unfamiliar places.

10. Express gratitude for the opportunity to have an adventurous career that combines your passions for travel and exploration.

Continue to visualize this scene regularly, adding more details and emotions that resonate with you. Allow yourself to feel the thrill and fulfillment that comes with having an adventurous job that takes you to exotic destinations. As you visualize, stay open to opportunities and take action steps that align with your career aspirations and travel goals.

To visualize having a loving husband and a fulfilling romantic life, you can follow these steps:

1. Find a quiet and comfortable space where you can relax and focus your attention.

2. Close your eyes and take a few deep breaths to center yourself.

3. Set the intention to visualize a loving and supportive relationship with your ideal partner.

4. Imagine yourself in a happy and loving relationship, surrounded by warmth and affection.

5. Visualize your partner as a kind, caring, and loving individual who cherishes and respects you.

6. Picture yourselves engaged in meaningful conversations, sharing laughter, and creating beautiful memories together.

7. Feel the love and emotional connection between you and your partner, allowing yourself to experience the joy and happiness that comes with a fulfilling romantic relationship.

8. Visualize moments of intimacy, trust, and support, where you feel deeply understood and valued by your partner.

9. Imagine going on romantic dates, sharing adventures, and supporting each other's dreams and aspirations.

10. Express gratitude for the loving partner and fulfilling romantic life you have visualized, feeling grateful for the love and happiness that fills your life.

Continue to visualize this scene regularly, focusing on the emotions and experiences you desire in a relationship. Trust that by visualizing and aligning yourself with your desires, you are attracting the right partner and creating the foundation for a loving and fulfilling romantic life. Remember to also take action steps and be open to opportunities that come your way to manifest the relationship you desire.

Once we have desired something, it is important to let it go and not cling to its manifestation. The more we obsess over its realization, the more we delay its arrival.

It may seem counterintuitive, but by releasing our attachment to the outcome, we create space for it to effortlessly flow into our lives.

When we become fixated on a desire, we often generate feelings of lack and impatience. This mindset creates resistance and blocks the natural flow of abundance and manifestation. Instead, we should trust in the process and have faith that what we desire is already on its way to us.

By detaching from the outcome, we free ourselves from the burden of constantly seeking and chasing. We shift our focus from a state of wanting to a state of allowing. This opens up the possibility for unexpected opportunities and synchronicities to unfold, bringing us closer to our desires.

Moreover, when we let go of the attachment to a specific timeline or way in which our desire should manifest, we invite the universe to work its magic in the most divine and perfect way. The universe has a greater perspective than we do, and by surrendering control, we allow for the highest good to manifest in our lives.

So, as we set our intentions and visualize our desires, let us also cultivate a sense of trust and surrender. Let go of any desperation or impatience, and have faith that what we seek is already in the process of manifesting. By embracing the present moment and being open to receiving, we create an energetic alignment that attracts our desires effortlessly and in divine timing.

Let's say you desire a fulfilling and harmonious romantic relationship. After setting your intention and visualizing your ideal partner, you release any attachment to the outcome and trust that the universe will bring the right person into your life at the perfect time.

You focus on cultivating self-love, nurturing your own happiness, and being open to new experiences. Instead of obsessively searching for a partner or feeling anxious about being single, you embrace the present moment and trust that the universe is orchestrating everything for your highest good.

You let go of any limiting beliefs or past relationship patterns that no longer serve you. You affirm positive statements like, "I am deserving of a loving and supportive partner," "I am open to receiving love," and "I trust that the right person will come into my life."

As you go about your daily life, you maintain a positive and open mindset. You engage in activities and hobbies that bring you joy and fulfillment. You radiate confidence and love, attracting positive energy into your life.

You detach from the outcome and avoid fixating on finding a partner. Instead, you focus on becoming the best version of yourself and living a fulfilling life. You have faith that when the time is right, the universe will bring a loving and compatible partner into your life.

By letting go of the need to control or force the process, you create space for divine timing and allow the universe to bring you a relationship that exceeds your expectations.

Remember, the key is to trust, surrender, and maintain a positive mindset as you align your energy with your desires. This approach allows the universe to work its magic and manifest your desires in the most beautiful and unexpected ways.

V

Time is an interesting aspect of our journey towards manifesting our desires. It can feel both like a friend and a foe, depending on our perspective and level of patience.

On one hand, time can seem like a barrier that separates us from our desires. We might feel frustrated or impatient when our dreams don't manifest as quickly as we'd like. We might question if our desires will ever come true, wondering when the waiting will finally end.

However, it's essential to remember that time is not an enemy working against us. Instead, it is a valuable teacher and a necessary part of the manifestation process. Time allows us to grow, learn, and evolve, preparing us for the fulfillment of our desires.

Rather than perceiving time as a hindrance, we can view it as an opportunity for personal development and self-discovery. We can use this time to cultivate patience, trust, and faith in the unfolding of our desires.

It's important to remember that the universe operates on its own timeline, which may not align with our immediate desires. Trusting the timing of the universe means surrendering control and embracing the present moment. It means acknowledging that there might be lessons to learn, experiences to gain, or inner work to do before our desires can fully manifest.

By shifting our perspective and embracing the journey, we can find joy and growth in the waiting period. We can use this time to align our energy, clarify our intentions, and continue taking inspired action towards our goals. In doing so, we create a fertile ground for our desires to flourish when the timing is perfect.

Remember, time is not an obstacle but an integral part of the manifestation process. Trust in divine timing and have faith that the universe is working behind the scenes to bring your desires to fruition. Embrace the journey, stay aligned with your intentions, and allow the unfolding of your dreams to happen in its own divine timing.

In the realm of desires, the concept of time can take on a different aspect compared to our everyday experience. While in the physical world time is often perceived as a linear measure, in the realm of desires it can be more fluid and flexible.

In the realm of desires, time is influenced by our vibration, focus, and connection with the universe. When we are in a state of alignment and trust, time can appear to accelerate, causing our desires to manifest more quickly than we expect.

On the other hand, if we harbor doubts, fears, or resistance, time may seem to elongate and our desires may take longer to manifest. This occurs because our energy and focus are not fully aligned with what we desire, creating a slowdown in the manifestation process.

It is important to emphasize that time in the realm of desires is subjective and can vary from person to person. The key lies in cultivating a strong belief in the timing of our desires and maintaining a state of alignment and positive expectation. By doing so, we can navigate the realm of desires with a greater sense of flow and ease, allowing our desires to unfold in their own perfect timing.

In the context of desires and manifestation, the term "vibrate" refers to the energetic frequency or resonance that we emit. Everything in the universe, including our thoughts, emotions, and beliefs, carries a specific vibration.

When we talk about "vibrating" at a certain frequency, it means aligning our thoughts, emotions, and beliefs with the desired outcome or state we want to manifest. It involves embodying the energy and feeling as if our desire has already been fulfilled.

For example, if we want to attract abundance into our lives, we need to vibrate at the frequency of abundance. This means feeling grateful for what we already have, having positive beliefs about money, and embodying a sense of prosperity and abundance in our thoughts and actions.

By consciously raising our vibrational frequency to match the desired outcome, we create a resonance with that reality and attract it into our lives. It's about aligning our energy with what we want to manifest and becoming a vibrational match to it.

In essence, vibrating refers to aligning our thoughts, emotions, and beliefs with the energy and frequency of what we desire, allowing us to attract and manifest those desires into our reality.

One way to accelerate the manifestation process is to cultivate a strong sense of belief and trust in the process itself. Trust that the universe is working in your favor and that your desires are on their way to you. Here's a suggestion to help you:

1. Affirmations: Create powerful affirmations that reinforce your belief in the manifestation process and the speed at which your desires are coming to you. Repeat affirmations such as:

   - "I trust that my desires are manifesting quickly and effortlessly."

   - "Every day, I am getting closer to the realization of my desires."

- "I am open and receptive to the rapid manifestation of my dreams."

2. Letting go: Practice the art of detachment and surrender. Trust that the universe knows the perfect timing for your desires to manifest. Release any resistance or attachment to the outcome and have faith that everything is unfolding in divine timing.

3. Gratitude: Cultivate a deep sense of gratitude for what you already have and for the manifestation of your desires. Express gratitude as if your desires have already manifested. This shifts your vibration to one of abundance and attracts more of what you desire.

4. Visualization: Engage in regular visualization practices, vividly imagining and feeling the reality of your desires already being fulfilled. Visualize the details, emotions, and sensations associated with the manifestation. This strengthens your belief and aligns your energy with the desired outcome.

5. Inspired action: Take inspired and aligned action towards your desires. Listen to your intuition and follow any guidance or opportunities that come your way. Trust that your actions, combined with the energy of belief and alignment, accelerate the manifestation process.

Remember, each person's manifestation journey is unique, and it's important to find techniques that resonate with you personally. Stay consistent, remain positive, and trust the process as you accelerate the manifestation of your desires.

Living in the here and now means being fully present and aware of the present moment, without being distracted by the past or worried about the future. It means tuning in to the present experience, accepting it without judgment, and allowing each moment to unfold fully. Here are some key concepts associated with living in the here and now:

1. Mindfulness: Being conscious of the present moment and intentionally paying attention to your thoughts, feelings, and sensations.

2. Letting go of the past: Releasing attachments to past experiences, regrets, or resentments and focusing on the present.

3. Non-judgment: Observing the present moment without labeling it as good or bad, right or wrong. Embracing a sense of acceptance and openness.

4. Gratitude: Cultivating appreciation for the present moment and recognizing the blessings and joys in your life.

5. Being fully engaged: Immersing yourself in what you are doing, whether it's work, relationships, or hobbies, with a deep sense of focus and presence.

6. Acceptance: Embracing things as they are, acknowledging that life is constantly changing, and finding peace in the present circumstances.

Living in the here and now allows us to experience life more deeply, enhance our relationships, reduce stress, and find greater joy and contentment in the present moment.

In conclusion, the power of affirmations and visualization lies in their ability to align our thoughts, beliefs, and emotions with our desired reality. By consistently repeating positive affirmations and vividly visualizing our desired outcomes, we activate the creative forces within us and attract the experiences and circumstances that align with our desires.

Remember, the key is to truly believe in the power of your thoughts and intentions. Embrace the idea that if you can imagine it, if you can feel it in your heart, then it is already yours. Trust in the process, have faith in your own power to manifest, and let go of any doubts or limitations that may arise.

As you cultivate a daily practice of affirmations and visualization, stay present in the here and now, appreciating the journey as much as the destination. Embrace the joy and excitement of co-creating your reality with the universe, knowing that each thought, each visualization, and each inspired action brings you closer to the fulfillment of your desires.

May this book serve as a guide and a reminder that you are the author of your own story, and through the practice of affirmations and visualization, you have the power to create a life filled with abundance, joy, and fulfillment. Trust in yourself, trust in the process, and trust that the universe is conspiring to bring your dreams into reality.

Now, go forth with confidence, clarity, and unwavering belief. Embrace the infinite possibilities that lie within you, and watch as your desires manifest before your eyes. Remember, if you can dream it, you can achieve it. Your destiny awaits.

Table of Contents:

By the same author, we have:

- I've changed my life

- Words that heal

- Unleashing Your Full Potential

- Shipping the future

Traduction in the world

Ruth Byrnes

Ruth Byrnes is a renowned writer and teacher specializing in the law of attraction. With a deep understanding of spiritual principles and the dynamics of the universe, Ruth has devoted her life to sharing the transformative power of the law of attraction with others.

Through her inspiring books and engaging seminars, Ruth guides individuals towards the realization of their dreams and goals. Her profound wisdom and practical techniques empower people to harness their thoughts, emotions, and beliefs to manifest their desired outcomes. Ruth's teachings have touched the lives of many, helping them unlock their true potential and create a life of abundance, joy, and fulfillment.

With her compassionate and empowering approach, Ruth Byrnes continues to inspire and guide others on their journey to manifesting their desires and living their best lives. Her insights and teachings are a beacon of light, illuminating the path to personal transformation and unlimited possibilities.

Printed: July 2023

www.ingramcontent.com/pod-product-compliance
Lightning Source LLC
Chambersburg PA
CBHW051218160726
47994CB00002B/649